The Dark Side of My Mind

Volume 9

Briana Blair

The Dark Side of My Mind Volume 9

ISBN 978-1-257-05624-8

Contact me: webmaster@bluedragoncreations.com

Visit my website: http://bluedragoncreations.com

Table of Contents

Volume 9

Poems 321 - 360

I Am Hell - *October 2010*

Clawing

Digging

Scratching upwards

Out from the rubble

I hid myself

Denied myself

And my power

Fuck that

I am Hell

And I am ready to rain down

Nuclear fucking fallout on your ass

I can't do it?

Watch me bitches

I'll swallow the world

And spit it out

The time for this Goddess

Has come

Tremble - October 2010

Tremble

And Worry

For Hell hath no fury

Like a bitch tied down

Held back under ground

I reveled in the pain

I'll never be the same

I've drawn my strength

From the width and the length

Of the hell you put me through

It's all because of you

So bow and pray

That you might be saved

From the Devil you made me

And the power you gave me

So tremble

And Worry

For Hell

Hath

No

Fury...

I'm There - February 2011

Thrust

Lust

Throbbing

Probing

Light

Strobing

Suck

Fuck

Just my luck

Kinky freak

Tongues seek

Desire

On Fire

Taboo

But you

Don't Care

And I'm there

Hate Set Me Free - February 2011

Break the chains

And shed a tear

No longer choking

On those fears

Stabbed my heart

Ran it through

But now I'm free

Without you

You sought to destroy

To wound and maim

Buy you made me the winner

Of this game

You've set me free

I can let it go

The gift you've given

You'll never know

I spent so long imprisoned

But couldn't see

Now the hate you've given

Has set me free

I Called - February 2011

I feel you

Inside me

Scraping off

The filth of ages

Peeling off

The old paint

Revealing

The beauty below

You guide me

Push me

Slowly out

Into the light

I called

And you answered

Mother

Father

teacher

God

Devour No More - February 2011

Come closer

Dig into me

Crawl inside me

And stay a while

I let you

Parasite

Feed off of me

Suck my life out

Use me

Consume me

Why couldn't I see

I was infested

Being digested

Consumed

By you

And all your kind

But no more

I pick you off

And stamp you out

Filthy little leeches

Devour me no more

Death Shell - February 2011

There's an itch

Like ants beneath my skin

Bone shift aching

This body is a death shell

Obscuring the real me

I want to claw, rip, tear

Peel it all away

And expose my real self

I feel sick

I'm dying in this flesh cage

I'm going mad in here

I need to get out

I have to get out

I can't die like this

Hunger Lust - February 2011

The hunger lust grows

Blood pumping fire

The beast strains

Hot sweet flesh scents

Tasty little morsels

Ripe for the picking

Night stalking soundless

The predator strikes

Fang rip crimson gush

Salty warm life flows

Drink deep and feel the power

The burning need satisfied

Then a sound

And I awake

But the nightmare continues

Soul Mingling Rush - February 2011

A kiss

Velvet lips

Tongue tracing

Salt sweet flesh

Warmth

Raven feather hair

A touch

Passion

Breath hitching

Soul mingling rush

Hunger

Lust

taste

And Touch

And make you mine

Deep Inside - February 2011

You're inside me

You crawled in

Deep under the skin

Burrowing deep within

Spider tendrils searching, seizing

You've been inside

Leeching, feeding

Making me sick

Making me a monster

I try to pull you out

Burn you, kill you

But I keep finding more

What will it take

To clear you out forever?

Artistic Flow - February 2011

I feel the flow

Colors, lines

Taking form

The ugliness

The beauty

The fear

The laughter

Born through my fingertips

And given to the world

Thoughts and feelings

Become reality

And when they are shared

They have life

Let it Flow - *February 2011*

Let go

Let it Flow

Soon enough I'll know

Silent words are spoken

Barricades are broken

Now the past is gone

I can finally move on

My potential is rising

With each demon I'm excising

So I let it go

Let it flow

Soon enough you'll see

The wonder inside me

Finally set free

Jot, Jot, Jitter* - *February 2011

Roughly sharpened pencil touch

Scratch, scratch, scratching

Mad woman scribbling

Thoughts surging, flooding

Hands can't move fast enough

Brain constantly a jumble

Searching for the words

Scribble, scribble, hen scratch

Figure it out later

Write it down, get it out

Jot, jot, jitter

Lipstick on the shower walls

A million thoughts spinning

Release upon the paper surface

'Til the feeling comes again

Nightmare Creep - February 2011

Creep, creep

While you sleep

Slink, crawl

Scratch the wall

Freak, fright

In your head

Little red eyes

Under your bed

Scary, scary

Things get hairy

Drift, dream

Make you scream

In the darkness

I sneak and creep

To scare you to death

Is what I seek

Rapist - ***February 2011***

Hold, push, penetrate

Your pattern doesn't deviate

Power, pain, maintain control

Fear and tears that you behold

Make a victim

With your crime

Plead innocent

Every time

For the evil

That you do

Someone should

Surely kill you

Evil scum

Your time will come

When you will pay

For the game you play

***Lost No More** - February 2011*

We've lost contact

With nature

With the spirit

We're out of touch

We act like we're alone

Feeling so lost

We need to reach out

Make contact again

Feel the beauty of nature

Feel the love of the spirit

When we do

We're lost no more

What Am I? - ***Started ?, Finished February 2011***

I don't know what I am

I'm hot with pain

Cold with fear

Hard with loneliness

Soft with need

I long for arms to hold me

Afraid of words that scold me

I need you

I hate you

I love you

I'd kill you

I understand

I'm confused

I need love

But I'm abused

I don't know who I am

I rage with anger

I embrace with love

I cower in worthlessness

I shine in pride

Fuck you all for doing this to me

Left to Give - *Started ?, Finished February 2011*

My body tingles

And yet there is a numbness

Caused by the knowledge

That all I ever was is lost.

And I am nothing

But was I ever anything?

I've accomplished no notable tasks

And though I thought I'd given

much in the ways of love

It seems I've touched no hearts.

To those I know I am a nuisance

Unpleasant and undesirable

More like a chore

Something that must be dealt with

On occasion.

My can no one see

Who I truly am,

All that I have given

And all I have left to give?

Woman Reborn - Started ?, Finished February 2011

See this face

So beautiful in its pureness and simplicity

See the child

Embodied by the innocence

See the woman

Given life through sensuality

See the pain

From her troubled youthful years

See the triumph

Of how she overcame adversity

See her blossom

See her grow

See the fear fall away

See her rise with grace

See her in a new light

See how much she's changed

See the woman be reborn

Eyes Upon Me - Started ?, Finished February 2011

Their eyes are upon me

Staring

Piercing

Seeing in

Or looking through

Never can tell

But they don't see

Judging

Leering

Condescending

Vision skewed

Too jaded

Want to stab their eyes out

Fools

Haters

Hypocrites

Ought to take a mirror

Look at yourself

Judge that

See yourself

Fears

Flaws

Lies

Bastards

Blinded - *Started ?, Finished February 2011*

Don't pretend to know me.

You know nothing of the truth.

You're blind to the facts.

Blinded by the lies you learned,

And the lies you tell.

You don't know me.

You don't even know yourself.

What gives you the right?

How dare you judge me?

How dare you tell me what I am?

You don't look beyond the surface,

Or care about the reasons.

Blind leading the blind,

Sharpened pitchfork in hand.

You don't know me.

You've never really seen me,

Never cared to really know.

You're blinded by hate,

By insecurity and jealousy.

Open your eyes for once.

Take a good look at yourself,

Then take another look at me.

Maybe then you can know me.

Organized Religion - Started ?, Finished February 2011

The sound is the same

Again and again

Parrot sounds

Repeated thoughtlessly

Can you think for yourself?

Can you speak for yourself?

Falling like lemmings from a cliff

No thought of why

Silly little sheep

Bleating, following

Obey your master

No mind of your own

Sense and logic need not apply!

Blind as bats

Dumb as stumps

We're right and you're wrong!

Blankly citing verses

Never question

Never think

Brains turned off

Free will on vacation

What a senseless waste

Dark Inspiration - *Started ?, Finished February 2011*

Sorrow and pain

Are the wells from which

My talent was drawn

For so many years

Happiness gave no inspiration

And I dreamed to be brighter

To speak of sunshine and grace

But pain is my power

And I've learned to embrace it

For it has made me grow

And blossom

Even in the darkness

It made me who I am

And who I am

Is beautiful

Stronger than you know

More wonderful than you imagine

The darkness made me see

The pain made me feel

The memories drive me on

So I embrace the shadows

And my dark inspiration

For they give me power

And strength

And hope

Best of Both - *Started ?, Finished February 2011*

I'm a pretty woman

Can I be your man?

Hard and rough

Or soft and sweet

I can be that, yes I can

Dazzle in the darkness

Sparkle in the light

Give it to ya honey

I can go all night

Take a good look

Size me up

Come on over

Fire me up

I'm the best of both worlds

A treat to meet

I'm your God and your Goddess

From my head to my feet

Masculine

And feminine

I'm the best

Of both of them

Don't know what you're missin'

Want a taste today?

Have a tumble baby

Don't let me get away

Too Much for You - Started ?, Finished February 2011

Why are you so quiet so suddenly?

Have I frightened you?

Am I too strong for your liking?

Too bad fucker

This is me

Brash and hard

Tough and unflinching

Oh, you don't like that do you?

Poor baby

You can't break me

Go on, keep trying sweetness

You'll just wear yourself out

Worse than you have tried

And better than you have failed

I'm too much a bitch

To be taken down that easy

So just shut up

Get the fuck out of my way

I'm too much woman for you

***Don't Let it Get You Down** - Started ?, Finished February 2011*

Don’t let it get to you

The pushing

Shoving

Beating

Crying

The talking

Faking

Whining

Lying

Rise above it

Start fighting

Trying

Rising

Shining

Fight harder

Loving

Sharing

Growing

Don't let it get you down

***Your Pathetic Reality* - Date Unknown**

I laugh

At your pathetic idea of "reality"

Mine is so much better than yours

In mine I can do anything

Be anything

Overcome everything

I have no limitations

There is no ceiling in my world

No mountain too high

And no river too wide

Your reality is so small

I feel so sad for you

Dream, fool

Open your mind

Expand your reality

Soar with the eagles

Reach for your dreams

Liquid Courage - Date Unknown

Oops

Made a mistake

Too much whiskey

Too much wine

Stumbling round

Reaching blind

Lost my mind

Nah, I'm good

Just one more

Here let me pour

Aw shit

I got talking

Told you what I really thought

Oops

Big mistake

Well fuck if you don't like it

Liquid courage worked

Gimmie that bottle

And shut your trap

Jackass

Only mistake

Was not starting on the bottle sooner

Evil Grandmother - Started ?, Finished February 2011

What a wicked game you play

When you talk to me this way

You say it's love but it's just lies

You have the wool over my eyes

You lock me up to show you care

And say that I should be happy there

Behind a door for no one to see

The sad little embarrassment that is me

You made me sick, you made me cry

You hoped that I would never try

Then came a day I decided to fight

A time when I knew it wasn't right

Then I chose to take my power back

It was I who made the next attack

It was never love you gave to me

And now I can clearly see

No longer your slave, No longer in fear

Everything's uphill from here

Games to Play - **Date Unknown**

I should stay in bed

There's so much evil

In my head

I should run away

So many mean games

I want to play

I should stay inside

And tell all my demons

They need to hide

I should be nice

And not give them a reason

To ever think twice

No

I should go and run

Scaring the little children

Would be such fun

I should kill to scream

And give them scary things

Of which to dream

No Tomorrow - February 2011

Insane

Rain

Missed the train

Out of this fucking life

Why go through so much strife

Used

Abused

Nothing to Lose

All the anger and the fear

There's just nothing left here

Insane

Rain

Too much pain

All the worry and the sorrow

I pray there will be no tomorrow

Nature's Song - February 2011

Blue sky flying

Floating, diving

Cotton cloud whispers

Freedom

Green grass running

Leaf soft unbound

Spring flowers laughing

Beauty

Tall tree dancing

Swaying, bending

Soft earth beckons

Experience

I Beg of You - February 2011

Change it

Change it all

I beg of you

I surrender

Show me the path

I'll walk it

Tell me the rules

I'll comply

just stop this

Stop the pain

Stop the sadness

Give me a reason

Show me the light

Give me hope

I beg of you

All My Life - February 2011

So many years

Tortured, trying

Working, Slaving

Seemingly for nothing

All my life

Scraping, begging

Needing, wanting

But getting nothing

So many nights

Dreaming, wishing

Crying, aching

Without an answer

Day after day

Hoping, praying

Struggling, fighting

What did I do to deserve this?

Fuck You to the World - February 2011

You thought I'd be dead by now

You never thought I'd be so strong

Or live so long

So yeah, my life's not great

But I'm living it

Every day is another fuck you to the world

Because suicide is the coward's way out

it would only prove I was a loser

Like you always said I was

But I'm not a loser

And I intend to live long enough

To make you eat every evil word

So fuck you

I Am in Love - February 2011

Lips

Sugar sweet

Gentle kiss

Fingertips

Silk soft

Fleeting touch

Hair

Feather soft

Flowing Gently

Eyes

Crystal blue

Subtle glance

Words

Softly spoken

I am in love

Lady Night* - *March 2011

The dark of night

Embraces me

Her ebony arms

Comfort me

Bat wings cross the sky

And wolves howl

How lovely is the night

In all her moonlit glory

Sheltering her children

From the light of day

Peace and love we find here

Her shadows give us peace

Within the Shadows - March 2011

In shadows walking

Unseen, unheard.

I wish it so.

Known only

To the creatures of the night,

For they do not judge.

They are as misunderstood

As I.

We must embrace the solitude.

Frightened minds

Refuse to see

The beauty

Within the shadows.

It Should Not Be So - March 2011

Oh how she rejoices

For a moment

In this new love

So beautiful and true

Then the smile fades

Shame sets in

And fear as well

It should not be so

Her heart has found

Such a perfect match

But that match

Is another woman

She tries to smile

And cling to joy

But they will not understand

And it should not be so

My Words, Your Guide - March 2011

Follow me tonight

It'll be alright

Let my words be a guide

To feelings you so often hide

Deep inside your pain and fear

You will find some solace here

In the things that we all feel

And sometimes wish weren't real

Through my words you may find peace

And acquire some sweet release

For I have been where you are now

You can get through, I'll show you how

www.ingramcontent.com/pod-product-compliance
Ingram Content Group UK Ltd.
Pitfield, Milton Keynes, MK11 3LW, UK
UKHW051134260726
13967UKWH00010B/3043

9 781257 056248